Neighbor Problems in India

By Siva Prasad Bose and Joy Bose

Published by Joy Bose

Copyright © 2022 Siva Prasad Bose and Joy Bose

All Rights Reserved

Contents

Dedication

Preface

1. Good neighbors and bad neighbors

2. Types of neighbor problems

3. Strategies to solve neighbor problems

4. Excessive noise and disturbances by neighbors

5. Illegal encroachment, trespass and construction by neighbors

6. Disputes related to utilities such as water and electricity

7. Threats, violence and harassment from neighbors

8. Problems related with kids and pets

9. Problems related with trees and plants

10. When Neighbors Make False, Unsubstantiated Allegations to Harass You

11. Conclusion

About the authors

Other books by Siva Prasad Bose

Appendix A: Glossary of Legal Terms

Appendix B: Quick Reference — Who to Contact for Common Problems

Dedication

This book is dedicated to all the residents of India and beyond who are suffering from the challenges of troublesome neighbors.

Preface

It is often said that we cannot always choose our neighbors. Sometimes, we are fortunate to have considerate neighbors who foster good relationships, creating a sense of community and mutual support. On the other hand, some neighbors may cause difficulties, making it challenging to live peacefully in our own homes.

In this book, we explore common problems with neighbors and provide practical strategies for resolving these issues. From noise disturbances to trespassing and harassment, we offer actionable steps to address these challenges. While the primary focus is on practical solutions, we also discuss legal remedies where applicable.

This book is tailored to the Indian context, addressing issues and legal recourses commonly encountered in Indian neighborhoods. However, many of these problems and solutions are universal and applicable across geographies.

Chapter 1: Good Neighbors and Bad Neighbors

We all have neighbors, some of whom we consider good and others bad. While bad neighbors can make our lives stressful and challenging, good neighbors can significantly enhance our well-being and happiness.

What distinguishes a good neighbor from a bad one? What are the benefits of having good neighbors? How severe can the problems caused by bad neighbors become? This chapter explores these questions and highlights findings from global surveys to better understand the scale of neighbor-related issues.

1.1 What makes a good neighbor?

Good neighbors are considerate, fostering a spirit of community by sharing joys, supporting each other in tough times, and respecting each other's boundaries. They avoid being excessively nosy or causing unnecessary disturbances.

Good neighbors are those who take care of their neighbors, who try to build a community spirit in the neighborhood, who share their joys and sorrows, and help and support their neighbors when they are going through tough times. They are not excessively nosy about their neighbors, do not try to trouble them and are mindful not to disturb them with too much noise or other inconveniences. They take the neighbors' permission or at least inform them if they have a celebration or party planned that might cause excess noise at late hours. At the end of any such party, they promptly clean up any trash left. They are mindful of the impact on their neighbors of any loud noises during construction and so on. In short, they are genuinely considerate of their neighbors and try their best not to let them have any kind of complaints.

Good neighbors go a step further by organizing community events, festivals, and activities that build trust and friendship. This not only enhances their own wellbeing but also contributes to a thriving neighborhood.

In the book "The Little book of Lykke" by Meik Wiking, the author, who is also the director of World Happiness Institute, cited the 2019 World happiness report by the United Nations Sustainable Development Solutions Network, which considered one of the factors in a country's happiness as the sense of community. It is the idea that we can rely on our neighbors to help us out in tough times.

Wiking suggests several ways to foster community spirit, such as:

- Creating a neighborhood directory to identify residents with skills, resources, or willingness to help.
- Establishing a book-lending cupboard or mini-library for shared reading.
- Developing public spaces for gatherings and conversations.
- Setting up a community garden.
- Starting a tool-sharing program to reduce the need for everyone to purchase the same tools.
- Hosting inclusive neighborhood events, ensuring no one feels excluded.

Having seen what makes a good neighbor and how one can consciously try to build a sense of community in the neighborhood, let us now discuss a few types of pressing problems with neighbors, based on some surveys taken.

1.2 Surveys on problems and attitudes towards one's neighbors

In this section, we consider a few surveys in some countries about people's attitude to their neighbors and the main types of problems with neighbors.

A 2019 Pew Research survey based in the US had the following findings:

- A majority of Americans (57%) say they know only some of their neighbors; far fewer (26%) say they know most of them

- Among Americans who know at least some of their neighbors, a majority (58%) say they never meet them for parties or get-togethers.

This survey showed that in this interconnected and modern world, we are getting more isolated and distant from our neighbors than, say, a generation or two ago. Similar trends probably hold for other countries like India.

Another 2017 survey of US households by homes.com website showed the following findings:

- 36% of the survey participants had disputes with neighbors that became full blown arguments.

- 1 in 4 had a long running feud with a neighbor.

- Top reasons for neighbor feuds included parking, general noise, trash or mess and animal noise.

- 40% of Americans were avoiding their neighbors, with top reasons being too busy, neighbors are too nosy, they are weird and that they didn't get along.

- 16% had moved their residence partly because of a neighbor and 20% were considering moving because of the neighbors.

A 2019 report by the Washington Post based on a survey by Porch.com revealed that the top four annoying activities of neighbors included being nosy, having loud parties, not picking up after their pets and parking in someone else's designated spot. Other problems included calling the police on their neighbors, leaving notes instead of speaking face to face, having loud sex, walking around without being properly dressed and having constructions that obstruct the neighbor's view.

A survey of UK households by the property website Goodmove found that only 17% of the people wanted to socialize with their neighbors, while 9% of the respondents did not want to communicate with the neighbors at all. Among the problems with neighbors, 64% of the people found loudness as the biggest problem, including 41% at loud children, 36% at loud pets and 25% at loud sex. Among other problems were nosiness at 53%, poor parking by neighbors at 52%, having a questionable lifestyle with possibly illegal activities at 49% and having lots of parties at 41%. Unapproved construction by the neighbors and poor garden or household maintenance were other problems mentioned in the survey.

Conclusion

This chapter highlights the qualities of good neighbors and the significant problems posed by bad ones. Global surveys reveal that neighbor-related issues are not uncommon, ranging from minor annoyances to severe disputes. Building a culture of mutual respect and community spirit can help mitigate these problems and promote a happier, healthier neighborhood.

References:

Penguin Books, Meik Wiking. The little book of Lykke. 2017.

SWNS Digital, September 6, 2021. Neighbors At War - Survey Shows Americans Really Dislike Their Neighbors https://swnsdigital.com/us/2017/10/heres-how-many-americans-have-full-blown-dispute-with-their-neighbors/

Leslie Davis and Kim Parker, Pew research, August 15, 2019. A half-century after 'Mister Rogers' debut, 5 facts about neighbors in U.S. https://www.pewresearch.org/fact-tank/2019/08/15/facts-about-neighbors-in-u-s/

Michele Lerner, The Washington Post, June 29 2018. What's The Worst Kind Of Neighbor? The Nosy Neighbor, Reveals Survey. https://www.ndtv.com/world-news/whats-the-worst-kind-of-neighbor-the-nosy-neighbor-says-us-survey-1875415

Goodmove, Nov 8 2021. Where to Find the UK's Worst (And Best) Neighbors?

https://goodmove.co.uk/blog/where-to-find-the-uks-worst-and-best-neighbors-good-move/

Chapter 2: Types of neighbor problems

Neighbors are an inevitable part of life; we do not choose them, but we must coexist with them. While most people maintain cordial relationships with their neighbors, disputes can arise on various issues, requiring us to address them thoughtfully. This chapter explores common neighbor problems, their impacts, and potential solutions.

2.1 Problems related to noise and disturbances

Noise and disturbances are among the most common complaints about neighbors.

There might be a party or celebration at the neighbor's house, with lots of people visiting and the noise of loud music continuing late into the night, not allowing us to sleep peacefully. Or else, there could be drilling or repair work going on at odd hours. The neighbors' electricity generator or some gadget or their TV could be too loud. They may be having a loud feud among themselves or with third parties.

Part of the problem, especially in case of apartments, can be that the walls in between the neighbor's apartment and ours could be too thin to weed out even noise if a little loud. Same goes for floors and ceilings as well.

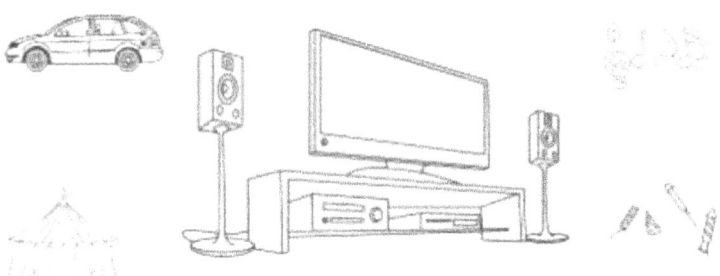

Figure: An illustration of neighbor problems related to excessive noise and disturbances, especially at odd hours of the night.

The visitors or guests of the neighbors may have parked in parking spots belonging to their neighbors, rather than the proper parking spots allotted to them. They may be drunk or rowdy and cause harassment in various ways. They may leave trash at common spaces or on the roads.

All of the above may also be done by the neighbors themselves, their tenants or their kids, rather than just visitors or guests.

2.2 Problems related to trespassing and access to property

Figure: An illustration of problems related to trespassing by the neighbors on one's property

Some neighbors might be frequently trespassing on our property. Others may construct illegal constructions or boundary walls or fences upon our property. Or else, they might install gates, locks or other mechanisms that obstruct our access to our own property. They might gradually over a few years if unchecked, trespass over the garden or common areas or non-residential areas until the whole area is taken over.

Similarly, in case of common doors or gates to the property, the neighbors may sometimes harass us by locking the shared gates, obstructing access to our own property. This may happen even during the daytime or when they do not need to be locked or when we are out of the house. In such cases, it may become a bother to request them to let us in when we are back, or needing to get a family member to open the common doors. This may be more of an issue in some multi-storied houses with a common entrance or exit for multiple apartments.

Damages property of neighbors

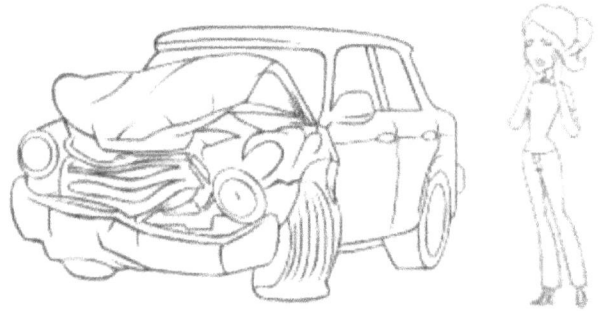

Figure: An illustration of neighbor problems related to damage of one's property, such as parked cars.

Another problem may be neighbors causing damage to our property, such as by cutting off trees, damaging cars or other items, damaging gardens, damaging existing boundary walls or gates and causing damage from ongoing construction work. Such damage may be caused sometimes by the neighbors' kids playing near the car park of the apartment and leaving scratches on the cars.

Such actions can lead to long-term disputes if left unaddressed.

2.3 Problems related to utilities such as electricity and water

In some cases, neighbors might be stealing or obstructing utilities such as electricity, water, gas and internet connections.

For example, **electricity theft** might be happening where the neighbors have secretly installed wires to illegally divert the electricity supply. This may end up with us facing huge bills while the neighbor enjoys free electricity stolen at our cost.

The neighbors may also, in some cases, tamper with the electricity supply, tamper with the meter or cut the wires to harass us.

The same may be true for **water theft**: the neighbor might have constructed a pipe or some other mechanism, unknown to us, to divert the flow of water provided by the city or municipality authorities. This would result in increased water bills for us and free use of water for them at our expense. Or else, they could be tampering with the water pump and pipes to obstruct our use of it. They may be in control of the common water tank to the building and cut off the water from the tank at random times, in order to harass and cause problems.

The problem may also be in the case of other **shared utility bills** such as Cable TV, Gas, Internet and so on. The neighbors may sometimes delay or refuse the pay their just share of the utility bills, in cases where there is a common connection to the property from the utility companies. This may lead us to be in a situation where we have to pay up or risk getting disconnected.

2.4 Problems related to flats in housing societies or apartment complexes

In housing societies or flat complexes, a number of people live in close proximity. Such a situation is different from that of individual houses. This can present unique problems. For example, the **noise may be amplified by thin walls or ceilings**. The neighbors may be leaving their trash in the common areas or not cleaning them. They may be encroaching on the common areas by making small constructions, or simply leaving their stuff like shoe racks in the common areas, reducing the available space for other apartments. Same can happen for other **shared amenities** such as garbage areas or play zones not being properly maintained.

2.5 Problems related to independent houses or villas

People living in independent houses can experience a different set of problems from their neighbors. These problems can include **boundary issues** and parking problems. For example, a neighbor may have encroached on their space or constructed a boundary wall or other illegal construction. There may be **security related incidents**, such as increased encroachments or incidents of thefts on the property if the owner is away for extended periods.

2.6 Problems related to housing associations

The housing associations are autonomous cooperative societies that take care of a certain residential complex such as a colony, block of flats, block of villas or independent houses. There may be multiple types of problems by such housing associations and their management, such as the following:

- Imposing **unnecessary or unjustified policies** and restrictions on the residents or their guests and visitors. This can include selective enforcement of guidelines.

- Imposing **discriminatory restrictions** on whether the owners are allowed to put their flats on rent, and what kind of people can be rented to.

- **Corruption**: such as mismanagement of funds for maintenance collected from the residents.

- Imposition of **additional and arbitrary fees** and charges on residents and tenants.

- **Denial of use of common facilities** such as recreation rooms, meeting rooms, parking areas and play areas for some residents or their guests.

- Not treating all flats equally but making priority policies for some flats whose owners are politically powerful.

2.7 Problems from neighbors related to violence and threats

Figure: An illustration of neighbor problems related to physical and verbal threats and violence

Figure: An illustration of a fight between two neighbors. AI generated art by Midjourney AI.

Some neighbors can be rowdy, threatening and cause violence and intimidation. Their intention might be to harass and persuade us to sell off our property at a cheap rate, or to persuade us to simply leave the property so that they can occupy it illegally.

The neighbors may also threaten our domestic servants such as house help, cooks and gardeners. Or else, they may obstruct our access to services such as home deliveries or mail by causing problems to the delivery persons.

Sometimes the neighbors may intentionally cut off communication, such as by refusing to take our calls or blocking our numbers, such that even speaking to them about the problems may become difficult. If we dare to ring their doorbell to communicate with them, they may attempt to intimidate or threaten us.

2.8 Problems from neighbors related to theft of moveable property

Our neighbors (or their visitors or tenants) can sometimes commit petty thefts on our property.

Figure: Thief breaking into a house. AI generated art by OpenArt AI.

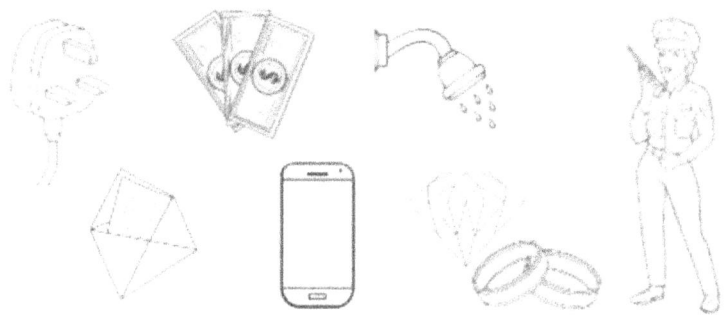

Figure: An illustration of neighbor problems related to petty thefts

Examples of things stolen can be tiny items kept in unprotected or common areas such as postal mail. It can include the daily newspapers or subscribed magazines. It can even go all the way to laptops, tools, gadgets and other valuables stored at our home, even vehicles. In cases when the owners are away on holiday or away for an extended period, such attempts of theft or break-ins by the neighbors may increase.

2.9 Problems from neighbors specific to senior citizens

Senior citizens often live alone and can be perceived as soft or weak targets by neighbors. There can be multiple cases of threats and harassment of senior citizens by the neighbors, due to varied motives such as snatching their property or harassment to persuade them to leave or sell the property for cheap. It can also include **obstructions and harassment** while doing simple daily tasks, or harassment of the helpers on whom the senior citizens depend on. It can also include obstruction in the use of common utilities such as electricity and water.

2.10 Problems from neighbors specific to women

Women if living alone might also be perceived as weak and soft targets. Apart from regular harassment and other issues, **sexual harassment** by neighbors or their visitors might be an additional problem. Unnecessary prying and **spreading rumors** about their lifestyles might also be a problem in some cases. This may also include **intimidation or coercion** in case of disputes.

Figure: Kids fighting in an Indian neighborhood. AI generated art by DALL-E AI art generator.

2.11 Problems from neighbors related to kids

There are multiple problems that could be to do with our own or neighbors' kids. Sometimes, our kids may get hurt when playing with the neighbors' kids in an unsafe areas, such as on the roof or near a muddy or slippery place. At other times, there may be a fight between two groups of kids and one's kids could get hurt.

The neighbors' kids could be bullying our kids. Sometimes, the neighbor adults could reprimand or hurt our kids. Other times, the neighbor kids could, while playing, leave scratches or damage our parked vehicles or other property. Similarly, the kids of the neighbors could be making too much noise and disturbing our peace. We need to have sensitivity and understanding when tackling such a variety of problems involving kids.

2.12 Problems from neighbors related to pets and plants

The neighbors' pet dog or cat could cause a nuisance in one's property by urinating or leaving poo, or could bite or scare the residents or their guests. This kind of harassment from pets could be due to them not being properly controlled by their owners.

Similarly, the neighbors' plants could be overgrowing on one's area or could be blocking the sunlight from one's window. There could be many other such problems. The neighbors could also intentionally damage our plants or obstruct the water supply.

2.13 Conclusion

Neighbor-related disputes can significantly affect one's peace of mind, security, and quality of life. Understanding these common issues is the first step in addressing them effectively. The following chapters explore practical strategies and legal remedies to resolve these   problems.

Chapter 3: Strategies to solve neighbor problems

Resolving neighbor disputes requires a calm, strategic approach. It is often best to start with friendly negotiations and escalate to legal remedies only when necessary. This chapter outlines various strategies to address common neighbor problems effectively.

3.1 Negotiations with the neighbors

The first step in case of any neighbor problems, before any legal or escalatory actions, should always be negotiations, in a friendly and cordial manner. This is by far the least effort, least stressful and cheapest way to resolve issues such as noise. In some cases, the noisy or troublesome neighbors might simply be unaware they are causing problems. Hence, simply explaining to them their specific behavior that is causing the issue and requesting them to stop it can work. This should be done as soon as the issue is detected and apparent and not much later.

Therefore, in case of any problems, we can try to have a quiet word with the neighbors, explain how their behavior is causing us trouble and gently request them to stop the behavior. This should be done as soon as possible after the incident happened or as soon as you notice a problem. Delaying might escalate tensions. This can be done either verbally or through a short letter or email or messaging, or some combination of these, along with details and photos or videos. We can repeat this negotiation strategy for at least two or three times before moving to further steps.

For example, in case there is too much noise in a neighbors' party in the night, next day we can inform the neighbors that the excessive noise made it difficult for us to get sleep. In case the neighbor is encroaching on our property or installed some construction materials, gently informing them to remove the material or remove the encroachments might work.

While informing the neighbors about the trouble their behavior is causing, we should not directly blame them, rather try to show them how their specific examples of behaviors are causing us specific problems. We should try to show empathy with their situation as well.

We can also try giving some positive incentives to the neighbors to motivate them to stop the troubling behavior, by showing willingness to help or cooperate if needed, such as assisting with a repair project or sharing tools.

During the negotiations phase, we should try to avoid getting into pointless quarrels or arguments. It is important to be calm and make our point firmly but peacefully and not allow the issue to escalate into an ugly situation, which is not beneficial to anyone, and might even make the original problem worse. It is especially important not to raise one's voice or to provoke the other party in any way when negotiating.

Figure: CCTV Cameras installed in a house. AI generated art by Midjourney AI.

It is better to install multiple CCTV cameras on our property for such kinds of problems. The CCTV cameras should be installed at strategic locations so as to cover different angles. Nowadays many outdoor (waterproof and weatherproof) and indoor CCTV cameras are available for reasonable prices of a few thousand Rupees on amazon and other shops. Such cameras often have features like real time monitoring and casting it via an app to one's mobile phone. The very presence of CCTV cameras can dissuade troublesome neighbors. They can be invaluable in collecting evidence which would be needed for any complaints or negotiations.

The following sections are for the cases where the peaceful negotiations fail to bring the desired behavior changes.

3.2 Complaint to Housing Society or Resident Welfare Association (RWA)

In India, as also in other parts of the world, for each apartment complex there is usually a housing society or cooperative association, or what is called Resident Welfare Association (RWA) in some cities. They can exist for different kinds of housing, including for a block of flats as well as a gated or ungated community of villas or independent houses.

Such associations have the responsibility of providing common services such as security or power backup to the residents of the community, as well as make policies about guests, parking, how to use the common rooms etc. It is also part of their responsibilities to maintain peace in the community and enforce general guidelines that are applicable for all residents.

In case of neighbor problems, we can escalate the issue to the housing association and request them for help. The issue can be raised in a written form or via messaging apps such as WhatsApp, which are commonly used for shared communication nowadays in RWAs and associations.

Here too, we should avoid language that sounds rude or blameful or generalizing, and instead write in neutral language and try to highlight the actual issue and the specific instances of the neighbors' behavior that are causing trouble. We can add details such as videos or photos or noise recordings as needed. We should be prepared to follow up with the association a few times, in case they are not taking any action.

Often, this raising of the issue to the association can have the desired effect of getting the neighbors to cease the problem behavior. Sometimes, the association may call for a face-to-face meeting with the neighbors to discuss and resolve the issue.

3.3 Complaint to the registrar of societies or consumer court

If the management of the housing society or association is itself the one causing the problems due to their policies or other actions, one can send a written complaint to the registrar of cooperative societies for the state or district of residence.

All housing associations and resident welfare associations (RWAs) are registered under the Societies Registration Act 1860.

The Societies Registration Act 1860 states the following:

6. Suits by and against societies: Every society registered under this Act may sue or be sued in the name of President, Chairman, or Principal Secretary, or trustees, as shall be determined by the rules and regulations of the society and, in default of such determination, in the name of such person as shall be appointed by the governing body for the occasion.

If the complaint is filed with the registrar of housing societies, they will issue a show cause notice to the chairman / president and secretary of the housing society. However, one needs to regularly follow up with them if any action has been taken on one's complaint.

Here too one should keep all the communication in written form and include all details as well as proofs if available. Also, one should include evidence of non-action by the housing association.

One may alternatively take the case to the consumer forum, court or police. One can also send a legal notice to the society or association management specifying the details.

3.4 Sending a Legal Notice

In some cases the neighbors, even after being warned repeatedly, continue with the instances of disruptive or troublesome behavior. In such cases we can try sending a legal notice to the neighbor to cease the action by a certain timeline, failing which further legal and other steps will be taken.

It is better to get the legal notice drafted by an advocate in our city on their official letterhead, and send it through a government run recorded post such as registered post or speed post. Include details of the issue, previous attempts to resolve it, and specific actions required to rectify the situation.

A sample legal notice has the following format (it is better to let the advocate draft it, below is only a guideline)

<Advocate's letterhead with the legal firm's name and address>

Through Registered Post/ Speed Post

Legal Notice

Date<>

To <complete name and address>

Dear Sir/Madam,

Under instructions from our clients <name and address>, we are instructed to address you as under:

That We/my client are/is the resident of <address of housing or flat> which is close to your property address of <neighbor address>.

That On <date and time>, you performed the following actions <specific details of the actions such as encroachment of property>.

That We had raised the issue on <date> verbally and via a letter, but despite the warning you did not <details of actions>.

That You are hereby instructed, by way of this legal notice, to perform the following corrective actions <list of corrective actions such as removing encroachments> within this date <date>

Failure to comply with this notice within the specified date will result in further legal actions to be taken against you as per the law. You will be liable for the costs of any such legal actions.

Yours faithfully:

<Signature and if possible, stamp of advocate>

Copy to: <Housing association>

3.5 Complaint to police

In case of some more serious issues, we can try to complain to the police through their number 100 or any of their hotlines in case of safety related issues, such as senior citizens hotline 1090 or women's hotline.

Again, the complaint can be a verbal or written complaint.

We should remember to jot down all the details of the incident, point by point, carefully before contacting the police. Also we should prepare and keep ready a list of evidence such as photos, videos, previous correspondence with the neighbors and previous complaints to police, housing association and other authorities.

Normally the police might send someone to our premises to conduct a preliminary investigation. If that does not happen, we can visit the police station to file a complaint, or e-file a complaint at the police website. If in spite of all our efforts, the police refuse or are unwilling to lodge a complaint, we can lodge a case in the court, which can order the police to file an FIR (First Information Report).

The figure below shows the webpage of a sample police website where one can lodge a complaint with all the necessary details.

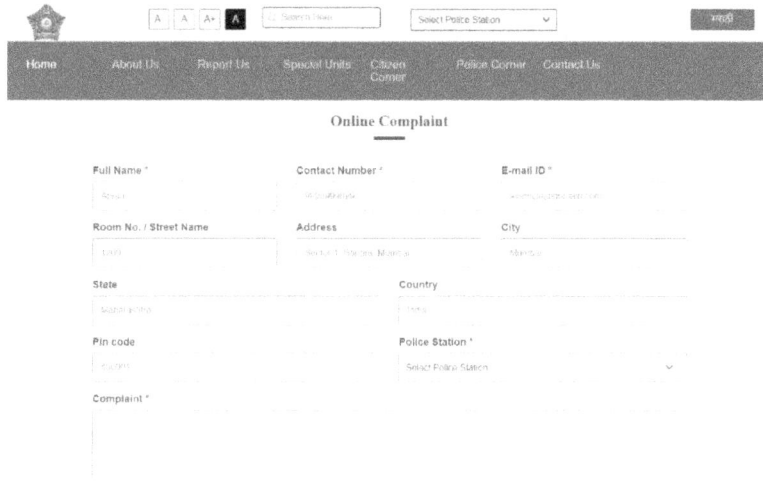

Figure: Police website of Mumbai police for lodging complaints online

3.6 Complaint to the local municipality

Sometimes the local municipality, which can be known by different names in India such as Nagar Nigam or Mahanagare Palike, might have a mechanism to lodge complaints in case of property or municipality related disputes.

We can visit the municipality or Nagar Nigam offices to file our written complaint in their complaint office. We can also file an e-complaint or write an email to them.

For example, the New Delhi Municipal council has a website (https://www.ndmc.gov.in/complaints.aspx) for lodging online complaints, shown in the figure below.

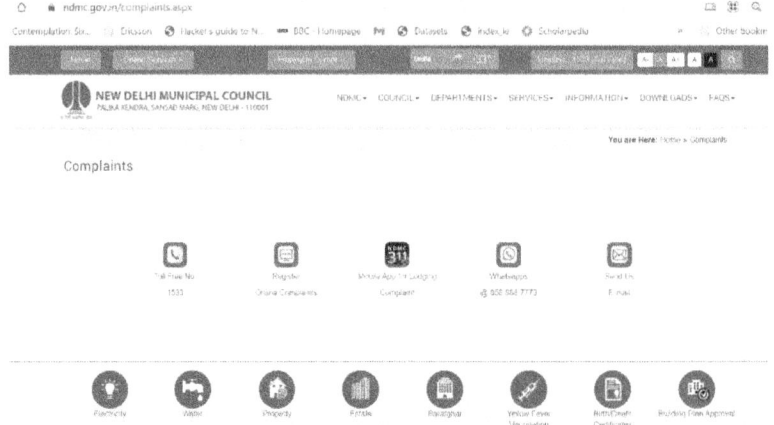

Figure: Webpage for lodging complaints at the New Delhi Municipal council

3.7 Complaint to the local MLA or MP or municipal corporators

In some cases, the MP or MLA or corporator might be able to help in case of small neighbor disputes in their area. We should visit their office or email them or write a formal written letter to them with the full details of the problem. Also, we can attend their public grievance redressal forums if available.

Often, the elected representatives such as MPs and MLAs have twitter accounts. We can tweet to them with the details of our complaints and ask for help.

3.8 Filing of a court case

In cases such as sudden property encroachments or forgeries or if the neighbor has not responded to our legal notices or warnings, we can file a court case in a local court. Such cases can take years to resolve under the Indian court system, so we should be mentally prepared and budget sufficient funds for this. We can do a cost benefit analysis as to whether it is worth the trouble and expense of taking the case to court.

We should engage a lawyer who is competent in such cases, and who ideally has prior experience in cases with this kind of disputes. The chosen lawyer should be conversant with email and modern means of communication, keep themselves updated with the latest laws and most importantly, listen to us carefully and act as per our instructions.

The normal court procedure involves the following steps:

- Filing of the case
- Sending notice to the defendants
- Framing of the issues by the court
- Hearing of arguments
- Presentation of evidence by both the opposing parties
- Cross examination

- Closing arguments
- Declaration of verdict.

If any party is not satisfied with the verdict, they may appeal to a higher court.

3.9 Conclusion

Resolving neighbor problems requires a judicious mix of diplomacy and legal action. Starting with friendly negotiations and escalating only when necessary can save time, money, and stress. The next chapters will delve into specific issues and detailed remedies for common neighbor problems.

Chapter 4: Excessive noise and disturbances by neighbors

Noise pollution is one of the most common complaints people have about their neighbors. Excessive noise, particularly late at night, can disrupt sleep, cause stress, and negatively impact health. This chapter explores the issue of noise disturbances and outlines steps you can take to resolve such problems.

Figure: Neighbors having a noisy party in their apartment at night. Image generated by Openart AI.

4.1 Indian Penal Code (IPC) and Bhartiya Nyaya Samhita (BNS) laws on excessive noise

Excessive noise comes under public nuisance as defined in section 268 and the punishment is stated in section 290 of the Indian Penal Code (IPC) and the corresponding sections in Bhartiya Nyaya Samhita or BNS. Section 268 is for causing annoyance to the public and can include, aside from noise, other kinds of annoyance such as threatening or denying public services to the public who lives in the area.

Section 268 of IPC on Public Nuisance states:

A person is guilty of a public nuisance who does any act or is guilty of an illegal omission which causes any common injury, danger or annoyance to the public or to the people in general who dwell or occupy property in the vicinity, or which must necessarily cause injury, obstruction, danger or annoyance to persons who may have occasion to use any public right. A common nuisance is not excused on the ground that it causes some convenience or advantage.

IPC Section 290 defines the punishment for causing public nuisance. It states as follows:

IPC 290 - *Whoever commits a public nuisance in any case not otherwise punishable by this Code, shall be punished with fine which may extend to two hundred rupees.*

Even though the amount of fine is negligible, the complaint might have the effect of dissuading the neighbor from repeating the loud noise in the future.

4.2 Noise pollution rules on excessive noise

The Noise Pollution Control and Regulation Rules 2000 also has provisions against noise pollution. It limits one's neighbors from playing loud music, bursting loud firecrackers or making any sound on a loudspeaker that goes beyond a certain limit (usually 10 Decibels) over the ambient noise in that area in the nighttime.

Nighttime is defined between the times of 10 pm and 6 am in this act. However, this is relaxed till midnight for festive or cultural occasions such as Diwali or Independence Day.

The Noise Pollution Rules 2000 state the following:

(1) The noise levels in any area/zone shall not exceed the ambient air quality standards in respect of noise as specified in the Schedule. (2) The authority shall be responsible for the enforcement of noise pollution control measures and the due compliance of the ambient air quality standards in respect of noise.

4.3 Steps to take when the neighbor is making noise in the night

If one's neighbor is making a loud noise or playing loud music, the first step would be to visit them and calmly request them to reduce the noise. Explain how their actions are disturbing you and propose solutions, such as lowering the volume during late hours.

One can also complain to the housing association or society and request them to speak to the residents of that flat for turning down the noise. Provide evidence, such as noise recordings, if possible.

If the above steps are not possible or if the neighbors do not listen and reduce the noise in spite of warnings, one can call the police by dialing 100/ 112. A visit from the police is usually enough to get one's neighbors to stop the noise.

One can file a police or court complaint against the neighbor on the basis of the following:

a) IPC section 290 and Bhartiya Nyaya Samhita (BNS) sections for public nuisance.

b) Noise pollution (Control and Regulation) Rules 2000 for exceeding permissible noise levels.

4.4 Conclusion

Excessive noise from neighbors can disrupt peace and well-being. While friendly communication is the preferred approach, escalating the matter to housing associations, police, or courts may be necessary for repeat offenders. Awareness of relevant laws and guidelines can empower you to address these disturbances effectively.

Chapter 5: Illegal encroachment, trespass and construction by neighbors

Encroachment occurs when someone occupies or uses property without the owner's consent. Neighbors may construct walls, fences, or gates illegally on your property, obstruct access, or cause damage through unauthorized activities. Such actions fall under the laws of trespass, which may involve both civil and criminal liability.

This chapter outlines remedies to address illegal encroachment and trespassing by neighbors.

5.1 IPC/BNS laws on criminal trespass

Trespass can be defined, in a legal sense, as follows: Trespass is an unlawful intrusion that interferes with a person or property. Specifically, it is a negligent or intentional act made by an individual that can cause injury to another person or their property without lawful justification, no matter how slight. It includes assault or threats made to a person, as well as trespass upon someone's property. The use of the term injury here means a violation of one's right and not actual physical harm or loss. Trespass to property includes trespass to chattels or moveable property as well as trespass to immoveable property. It typically applies to tangible property and allows the owners of such property to seek relief when a third party intentionally, carelessly or recklessly interferes or meddles with the owner's possession of such moveable or immoveable property.

Trespass of property is where someone illegally gains entry to and occupies the property that legally belongs to someone else, against their will. Trespass in case of property can be both civil and criminal. Criminal trespass is where the occupier threatens the owner of the property or commits violence. Where criminal trespass does not apply, it is civil trespass and comes under tort law.

All trespass may not be classed as criminal trespass, unless violence and intimidation are involved. If it is not criminal then civil remedies, such as a court case, may be applied.

There is also a trespass called house trespass where a person, such as a neighbor commits criminal trespass on a portion or whole of your house where you are currently staying.

Section 441 of Indian Penal Code IPC (and the corresponding section in BNS) deals with criminal trespass, and 447 for punishment for criminal trespass. Section 442 deals with house trespass.

Section 133 of IPC describes the procedure for removal of nuisances of illegal construction by neighbors.

The sections 441, 442 and 447 of IPC are discussed in the following subsections.

5.2 IPC 441 Criminal trespass

Whoever enters into or upon property in the possession of another with intent to commit an offence or to intimidate, insult or annoy any person in possession of such property, or having lawfully entered into or upon such property, unlawfully remains there with intent thereby to intimidate, insult or annoy any such person, or with intent to commit an offence, is said to commit "criminal trespass".

5.3 IPC 442. House trespass

Whoever commits criminal trespass by entering into or remaining in any building, tent or vessel used as a human dwelling or any building used as a place for worship, or as a place for the custody of property, is said to commit "house-trespass".

5.4 IPC 447. Punishment for criminal trespass

Whoever commits criminal trespass shall be punished with imprisonment of either description for a term which may extend to three months, with fine or which may extend to five hundred rupees, or with both.

5.5 How to deter someone from trespassing one's property when one is away

It is far better, cheaper and easier to deter the neighbors from trespassing rather than to get them to vacate once they have already trespassed the premises.

As we know, land where the owner is away for extended periods is particularly vulnerable to trespassing. So one can keep a "no trespassing" sign on the premises of the property. One can also build high boundary walls around the property with the notice for no trespassing painted on the walls. In addition, one could hire a security guard or pay the security guards of the area to keep a regular watch on one's property for cases of attempted trespass. One can also install CCTV cameras to monitor the premises remotely and keep a record of trespassing incidents.

5.6 What do to if someone trespasses one's property

If someone illegally occupies a part or whole of one's property, one can follow the following steps as applicable:

- Obtain photos, videos and other proof of the trespassed property. If the neighbor has made any illegal constructions on our property, get proof of that as well.

- In case of criminal trespass or trespass with threats and intimidation by the neighbors, visit the nearest police station and/or file a written complaint, asking for help and protection. Include documentation and proofs such as photos.

- Send a legal notice to the neighbor who has trespassed, asking them to vacate the illegally trespassed property, failing which legal proceedings will be initiated.

- File a lawsuit or writ petition before the courts (such as district court or high court) requesting direction to the police and other authorities for eviction of the occupier (neighbor who has trespassed) from the property and restoration of possession of that property to us.

- File a suit before the courts requesting to pass an immediate stay / injunction against any construction and/or sale of the illegally occupied property, and demolishing of any illegal construction already made by the neighbor.

- File a complaint to the municipal corporation (such as MCD in Delhi) against illegal trespass of our property by the neighbors, with proofs such as photos. This is also applicable if some construction has been made by the neighbors without proper planning permission.

- File a written complaint before the sub divisional magistrate (SDM) with proofs.

- File a civil suit for damages from the neighbors for illegal occupation of our property.

- File a complaint with the revenue or land authorities to prevent mutation of land records by the neighbors.

Note that the above steps include both civil and criminal trespass.

5.7 What do to in case of extended civil trespass

Civil trespass comes under law of torts. Tort means a civil wrong, i.e. where a person harms or violates the civil rights of another. In this case, the wronged person can file a court case on the other for compensation for damages and losses incurred by the wronged person.

In case of illegal occupation of property, actions such as building unauthorized construction on another's land or property, denying someone access to their own property, for example by installing locks or gates, would come under the definition of trespass and would fall under tort law. Hence, the owners of such property can claim recovery of damages from the occupier. The same holds where a neighbor builds fences, gates or other construction that encroaches one's property.

However, as mentioned earlier, if the illegal occupation is accompanied by threats or violence by the occupier, it would fall under the category of criminal trespass and a police complaint can be filed.

5.8 Adverse possession and civil trespass

One must be extra careful, in case of trespass, to take action promptly before it is too late. Under Indian law, if a trespasser has been in continuous control over a property for 12 years, without any legal action by the rightful owner to eject the trespasser from the property, it is termed as "**adverse possession**".

Extract from the Wikipedia article on adverse possession: "*In general, a property owner has the right to recover possession of their property from unauthorized possessors through legal action such as ejectment. However, in the English common law tradition, courts have long ruled that when someone occupies a piece of property without permission and the property's owner does not exercise their right to recover their property for a significant period of time, not only is the original owner prevented from exercising their right to exclude, but an entirely new title to the property "springs up" in the adverse possessor. In effect, the adverse possessor becomes the property's new owner.*"

The idea behind the adverse possession law is that if the rightful owner does not take any action to claim the property or take care of the property for the time period specified, the law assumes that they are not interested in the property and hence the trespasser can be awarded the rights.

However, it is to be noted that if the rightful owner starts court proceedings to eject the trespasser from the illegal occupied property before the 12 years of continuous occupation are over, then the time from the beginning of the illegal occupation would not be counted at all in the 12 years, as long as the legal proceedings are ongoing.

Therefore, if one's property is being trespassed by an illegal occupier, it is best to initiate the court proceedings as soon as possible.

It is best to ensure that illegal occupation does not take place initially. For this, the rightful owner should keep checking on it regularly to make sure that illegal construction is not being made on the property. They should, if needed, construct boundary walls on the property to deter illegal possession.

In India, illegal possession can be a major issue with NRIs who may be working for many years in a foreign country and not checking on their own land regularly. However, it may also happen due to unscrupulous relatives or others who may have designs on the property.

5.9 Conclusion

Illegal encroachments and trespassing by neighbors can be stressful and financially burdensome. However, timely action, proper documentation, and awareness of legal remedies can help resolve such issues. In the next chapter, we will discuss disputes related to shared utilities like electricity and water.

Chapter 6: Disputes related to utilities such as water and electricity

Disputes over utilities like water and electricity are common among neighbors, particularly in shared housing or apartments. These disputes can involve theft, tampering, or non-payment of shared bills, leading to financial and logistical challenges. This chapter outlines remedies for resolving such conflicts.

6.1 Theft or tampering of electricity supply

In case of suspected electricity theft or tampering of the electricity supply by the neighbors, the remedy is to call a competent worker such as an electrician and have them take a close look at our electricity connection. One can do this in case of faulty meter readings as well as cases of electricity supply disruption. In particular, one can request the competent electrician to examine if there are any wires going from our main electricity connection to the neighbor's house or flat where it should not be, or any such wires have been tampered recently. Or one can do a small test, turning off all the electrical appliances in that floor and then testing if the meter is stopped or is still running in spite of all appliances being switched off.

One should keep a record of any statements made by electricians and plumbers after examining one's electricity supply. Similarly, one should take photos and videos of any damaged wires and other equipment.

In case of such theft of electricity supply, one can file a complaint (either in person or online on their app or website) with the local electricity board or electricity supply company asking for an official technician to visit the premises and examine if the electricity is being diverted.

Once this is confirmed by the official technician, one can request them to give a signed statement of what is happening. On the basis of this statement, one can file a complaint with the police as well as the company that supplies electricity in one's city, such as BESCOM or DISCOM.

In case the electricity supply is tampered with by the neighbors, one can lodge a complaint using the BESCOM, BSES Rajdhani or similar electricity provider company's app or website. One can also lodge a complaint with the city's municipality office, such as New Delhi Municipal Corporation, reporting the same.

Since electricity and water are essential utilities, cutting the or damaging the supply is a criminal offence. Therefore, one can file a police report as well. One can call 100 or 112 and lodge an FIR with the police in case one's electricity supply is tampered or cut off. All calls to

112 are logged, so it is better to call this number and request the police constable to visit the premises and investigate.

Alternatively, one can send a legal notice to one's neighbor stating the date, time and details of the incidents and requesting them to cease and desist immediately, failing which further legal proceedings will be initiated against them.

Figure: Electricity supplier company in Delhi, BSES Rajdhani website to lodge complaints about problems such as electricity supply disruption and faulty meter readings.

Section 135 of the Electricity Act 2003 states the following:

Section 135. (Theft of Electricity): ---

(1) Whoever, dishonestly, --

(a) taps, makes or causes to be made any connection with overhead, underground or under water lines or cables, or service wires, or service facilities of a licensee or supplier as the case may be; or

(b) tampers a meter, installs or uses a tampered meter, current reversing transformer, loop connection or any other device or method which interferes with accurate or proper registration, calibration or metering of electric current or otherwise results in a manner whereby electricity is stolen or wasted; or

(c) damages or destroys an electric meter, apparatus, equipment, or wire or causes or allows any of them to be so damaged or destroyed as to interfere with the proper or accurate metering of electricity,

(d) uses electricity through a tampered meter; or

(e) uses electricity for the purpose other than for which the usage of electricity was authorised, so as to abstract or consume or use electricity

shall be punishable with imprisonment for a term which may extend to three years or with fine or with both:

6.2 Theft of water supply

For a suspected theft of the water connection, we can check if there are any pipes or any means by which the water connection to one's house or flat is being diverted to some other location such as the neighbors. We can similarly check for any blockages or obstructions to the supplies.

In case of water theft, one can file a complaint with the Jal Nigam or water board in their city municipality, along with relevant evidence such as photo or video evidence if available. Ask them to investigate by sending a competent person such as plumber to check our water supply. If possible, get a signed statement from them. Also, one can file a complaint with the police.

As per the directions of the National Green Tribunal, stealing or misuse of potable water is an offence punishable with a fine, and one can file a complaint at the Delhi Jal Board for the same.

It is good to always communicate in written form with government agencies such as the water boards or electricity suppliers. Similarly for every complaint raised with such agencies, one should try and get a complaint number from them, so one has a record of all previous complaints made. These complaint numbers may again be used to reference the past incidents with the neighbors, when complaining to other agencies like the police or when filing cases in the courts.

Figure: Website of the Delhi Jal Board, the company responsible for water supply in Delhi, listing the numbers and ways to contact them and lodge complaints.

6.3 Theft of other services such as gas, WiFi internet or cable TV

For theft of other services such as internet, first we should make sure our Wi Fi password is secure, in case of wireless services. In case of wired services, we can call the internet provider to investigate.

Similarly for Cable TV and other services, we can call the respective service providers and ask their help to investigate any suspected theft of the services.

The Information Technology (2000) Act deals with cyber crimes such as unauthorized stealing of internet usage. Chapter 9 of the IT act states the following:

43. 6 [Penalty and compensation] for damage to computer, computer system, etc.–If any person without permission of the owner or any other person who is in charge of a computer, computer system or computer network,– (a) accesses or secures access to such computer, computer system or computer network 7 [or computer resource];

(b) downloads, copies or extracts any data, computer data base or information from such computer, computer system or computer network including information or data held or stored in any removable storage medium;

(c) introduces or causes to be introduced any computer contaminant or computer virus into any computer, computer system or computer network;

(d) damages or causes to be damaged any computer, computer system or computer network, data, computer data base or any other programs residing in such computer, computer system or computer network;

(e) disrupts or causes disruption of any computer, computer system or computer network;

(f) denies or causes the denial of access to any person authorized to access any computer, computer system or computer network by any means;

(g) provides any assistance to any person to facilitate access to a computer, computer system or computer network in contravention of the provisions of this Act, rules or regulations made thereunder;

(h) charges the services availed of by a person to the account of another person by tampering with or manipulating any computer, computer system, or computer network;

(i) destroys, deletes or alters any information residing in a computer resource or diminishes its value or utility or affects it injuriously by any means;

(j) steal, conceal, destroys or alters or causes any person to steal, conceal, destroy or alter any computer source code used for a computer resource with an intention to cause damage;

he shall be liable to pay damages by way of compensation to the person so affected.

For suspected theft of utilities such as gas, it is a good idea to call and expert, preferably from the gas company, to have a look and verify first whether the theft is indeed happening. As always, do not forget to collect and store the evidence in form of photos and videos.

6.4 Theft of postal mail and other items

In case we suspect that our mail is being stolen by the neighbors, we can do a few steps:

- Set up CCTV cameras in strategic places to capture if the mail or other items are being stolen.
- Send a few dummy packages or post to actually verify if the theft is happening.
- Speak with the postman or courier person in our area to ascertain the exact circumstances.

Theft of mail is a cognizable offence under the Indian Post Office Act, 1898.

Section 69 of the Indian Post Office Act 1898 states the following:

69. Penalty for unlawfully diverting letters.- Whoever, not being an officer of the Post Office, willfully and maliciously, with intent to injure any person, either opens or causes to be opened any letter which ought to have been delivered, or does any act whereby the due delivery of a letter to any person is prevented or impeded, shall be punishable with imprisonment for a term which may extend to six months, or with fine which may extend to five hundred rupees, or with both.

Therefore, if one can prove, through CCTV, photos, videos or any other evidence, that theft of our mail by the neighbors is indeed happening, one can file a police complaint on that basis.

6.5 Refusal of neighbors to share the utility bills of common utilities such as electricity or water

Sometimes we may be living in an apartment complex or group of flats or independent house where the utility bills such as electricity or water are shared with the neighbors. Occasionally we may be unlucky to have a neighbor who refuse to pay their fair share of the water bill or electricity bill despite using it. In such cases, we may feel stuck because filing court cases for such tiny matters could be expensive and troublesome and simply not worth it.

In shared housing setups, disputes may arise when neighbors refuse to pay their share of common utility bills for electricity, water, or internet. This can lead to financial strain for the paying party.

Below are some actions we can take to get the neighbor to pay their share of the bill:

- Try to negotiate with the neighbors about the need to pay their fair share of the electricity or water bill. Carry the previous bills that are unpaid and proofs of your payment if any. This is the easiest and most preferable option. If despite repeated negotiations, they do not agree to share the bills, only then try the other steps.

- Separate out the meter readings of the utilities, such as by installing a sub-meter for the water or electricity that you are using. Persuade the neighbors to pay their fair part of the bill as per the readings of the sub-meter.

- Get a different and separate connection for the utility. Write a written letter to the Jal Board or Electricity board requesting a new connection.

- File a written complaint to the utility board about the nonpayment. Do get the evidence of your paying of the same first. Request them to come and intervene to get the shared payments.

- File a complaint with the local municipality or corporation about the non-payment by the neighbors. As earlier, always first keep a careful record of all bills and their receipt and enclose all the evidence of your paying the bills with the complaint.

- File a written complaint with the local police, local RWA or resident welfare association, local municipal authorities, and any other authorities about the non-paying of the shared bill and requesting them to intervene and help in the matter.

- Send the neighbors a legal notice from a lawyer stating the exact facts of the case and how much amount of money is pending from them. State clearly the interest they would be liable if they do not pay by a certain date.

- Try different complaint and recovery mechanisms that may be available for recovery of small amounts owed to you from another person.

- You could also try stopping all payments for the utility after giving them a written notice of non-payment by the neighbors. Eventually the utility could get disconnected due to non-payment which will affect you as well as the neighbors. However, make sure you have informed multiple authorities in electricity board or Jal board in writing multiple times before this happens.

- If all else fails, file a court suit to recover the pending amount. This should be the last resort but if you have to resort to this option, collect the full evidence and do your homework thoroughly and take advice from multiple lawyers on the best way to go about it, before starting any case.

6.6 Conclusion

Disputes over utilities can be frustrating and financially taxing. Understanding the legal framework and taking preventive measures, such as installing sub-meters and security systems, can help resolve these issues effectively. In the next chapter, we will explore problems involving threats, violence, and harassment from neighbors.

Chapter 7: Threats, violence, and harassment from neighbors

Some neighbor disputes escalate to serious issues involving threats, harassment, or even violence. These situations require immediate attention and appropriate action to ensure personal safety and peace of mind. This chapter provides guidance on how to address such problems.

7.1 Indian Penal Code / BNS sections relevant to assault and injury

Section 268 of Indian Penal Code IPC (and corresponding sections in Bhartiya Nyaya Samhita or BNS) states:

IPC 268. Public nuisance - A person is guilty of a public nuisance who does any act or is guilty of an illegal omission which causes any common injury, danger or annoyance to the public or to the people in general who dwell or occupy property in the vicinity, or which must necessarily cause injury, obstruction, danger or annoyance to persons who may have occasion to use any public right. A common nuisance is not excused on the ground that it causes some convenience or advantage.

Section 425 of IPC states:

IPC 425 (Mischief) - Whoever with intent to cause, or knowing that he is likely to cause, wrongful loss or damage to the public or to any person, cause the destruction of any property, or any such change in any property or in the situation thereof as destroys or diminishes its value or utility, or affects it injuriously, commits "mischief".

IPC 506 (Criminal Intimidation): Threatening someone to cause harm or fear of harm is punishable under this section.

These sections of the IPC can be used in the case of troublesome neighbors who cause too much noise and other disturbances. This can be the legal basis for us to get an injunction from the court against harassing neighbors.

7.2 Actions to be taken in case we are threatened or violently attacked by neighbors

The following are the actions that can be taken if we are being threatened by our neighbors, whether physically or verbally:

- File a regular complaint at the local police station or call 100.

- Send a legal notice to the person giving the threats with the help of a lawyer, asking them to cease and desist immediately, failing which legal actions will be initiated.

- In case of injury from violent actions from one's neighbors, collect evidence from the doctor's report at any government hospital and any photographic evidence of the injuries.

- We can also approach the higher police authorities directly with details of our complaint, such as the Senior Superintendent of police (SSP) or Deputy Commissioner of Police (DCP).

- We can file a complaint under Section 506 of Indian Penal Code: Criminal intimidation.

- Depending on the severity, we can file a non-cognizable (NC) complaint about criminal intimidation by our neighbors at the local police station.

- In case the police do not act on our complaint, which can happen if the neighbors are politically connected, we can raise a case in the courts asking them to order the police to file an FIR.

- Write to or meet the local MP, MLA, or corporator asking for protection and giving full details of the intimidation or violence by our neighbors.
- File an application with the local court asking for a restraining order against the neighbor who is threatening us.

If we act and report to the authorities promptly when the initial threats are given, they will prevent the situation from getting worse later.

Figure: A senior citizen complaining to the police officer in a police station in India. AI generated art by OpenArt AI.

7.3 Actions in case senior citizens or elders are threatened or attacked

The following additional actions can be taken if the persons who are threatened are senior citizens:

- Call the elders helpline of the local police (1090, 1091, 1291) and make a complaint. There may be a website or number of the senior citizens cell, if it exists in our city. If it exists, it is preferable to use the senior citizens cell, because they are specifically run for senior citizens and will give a more sympathetic and patient hearing.

- Often senior citizens charities and NGOs such as HelpAge India and Dada Dadi Organization run helplines in many Indian cities. Google or search if such a helpline is available. If there is such a helpline, we can call the helpline in our city and ask for help giving the full details.

- File a written petition at the local senior citizen tribunal (usually the additional district magistrate or SDM) giving details and asking for protection from our neighbors, under the Senior citizens protection act 2007.

- One important thing to note is to communicate everything in writing rather than verbally, to create a written record with the authorities. Senior citizens may tend to forget events if there is only a verbal record.

Figure: Website of the senior citizens cell of Delhi police

7.4 Actions in case women are threatened or attacked

Figure: Website of the National Commission of Women (NCW), where women can file a complaint

The following additional actions can be taken if the persons who are threatened are women:

- We can file a complaint at the National Commission for Women (NCW) cell in our city or state. The NCW website is shown in the figure above.

- In some cities, the local police might have a separate women's cell. We can file a complaint there.

- There may be charities or NGOs such as Vanita Sahayavani running in our city to help women. We may additionally complain to any of these charities.

7.5 Actions in case one's domestic helpers or servants are harassed by the neighbors

The following actions can be taken if one's neighbors are harassing and obstructing our domestic servants such as the gardener, house worker, maid, etc.

- Get a recorded written and verbal statement from our domestic servant who is being harassed.
- File a complaint with the police in addition to the other complaints of intimidation, with these statements.

The criminal case for harassment may be recorded with the police as per the concerned IPC sections. If the police do not act, the case may be registered at the court to force the police to lodge an FIR.

The same goes when one's delivery agents or postman or courier delivery persons are being harassed or obstructed or not allowed to perform their work by the neighbors.

7.6 Conclusion

Threats, violence, and harassment by neighbors are serious issues that require swift action. Filing police complaints, documenting evidence, and seeking support from legal or government authorities are essential steps to ensure your safety and resolve the matter. The next chapter will discuss issues related to children and pets.

Chapter 8: Problems Related with Kids and Pets

Children and pets are common sources of neighbor disputes. While their actions are often unintentional, they can cause disturbances or damage, leading to conflicts. This chapter explores common issues involving kids and pets and suggests practical ways to address them.

Figure: Kids playing and damaging one's car. Generated by Openart AI

8.1 Summary of problems related to neighbors' kids

The neighbors' kids could be causing different types of problems. They could be playing too loudly or playing loud music. They could damage one's property while playing, such as leaving scratches on one's parked car or breaking one's window with a cricket ball when playing cricket. They could be bullying one's own kids.

8.2 How to deal with problems involving the neighbors' kids

Kids are kids, so may not be aware of the consequences of their own actions. In addition, their behavior may have to do with their upbringing.

Hence, it is better to be sensitive when dealing with the neighbor's kids. One should gently but firmly warn the neighbors' kids not to make too much noise or not to damage one's property. Under no circumstances should one try to hurt the neighbors' kids.

If that does not work, or if incidents like bullying happen, one may approach the neighbors' kids' parents and request them to control their kids' behavior. It is better if both the husband and wife go for such discussions with the neighbors. However, one should be sensitive not to raise one's voice here and not to fight with the neighbors in front of the kids. Other tactics mentioned in the section on negotiation with the neighbors may also be used.

However, if negotiating with the neighbors about their kids' behavior does not seem to work, then one can approach the housing association and complain to them. One can also take measures so that one's property and one's own kids are protected and any incidents with the neighbors' kids do not happen again. Examples of such measures could be installing a higher boundary wall or proper gates fitted with CCTV. If none of these work, one can approach the police. However, approaching the police is not advisable and should only be done as a very last resort, since the kids are minors and hence not legally responsible. Also, such experiences can be traumatic for the kids involved.

8.3 Summary of problems related to one's own kids

There could be other kinds of problems related to one's own kids and the neighbors. One's kids may get hurt when playing with the neighbors' kids in an unsafe area or in a fight between two groups of kids. The neighbors' kids could be bullying our kids. Also, the neighbor adults could reprimand or hurt one's kids.

8.4 Solving problems related to one's own kids

Here too, the same tactics are advisable. One should talk to one's own kids first and get the details of any incidents in a calm way. After that, one can decide whether to escalate the problem to the one's neighbors.

One should be protective but not overprotective of one's own child and keep in mind that one's kids getting hurt is entirely possible when playing with others. If needed, one should keep one's child supervised at all times and not allow them to play in dangerous areas.

If one's kid has been hurt by the neighbors' kids, a simple apology from the kids may suffice. One may also request them to share some part of the medical bills if the kids have been hurt badly and needed to be admitted to the hospital, although it is a subjective matter and may not be likely.

If negotiations do not work, then the usual options of complaining to the housing association or to the police or in the courts may be tried, but only as a very last and extreme resort.

8.5 Solving problems related to pets

Pets such as cats and dogs could also be causing problems, whether it be one's own pets or the neighbors'. Here too the same principle applies: try to solve things by negotiation first. Keep proof, such as CCTV feeds of the neighbors' pets causing a nuisance on your property.

There are certain applicable laws related to pets. Animals are normally protected under Prevention of Cruelty to

Animals Act, 1960. Problems with animals can be reported to the animal welfare board.

One should make sure one's own pets and the neighbors' pets are following the laws. In particular, dogs should not be free to run around unless on a leash in common areas, where they can bite and hurt people. It is the responsibility of the owners to keep dogs on a leash and they are liable for any damage caused by their pets.

In case one has been bit by a neighbor's dog and in need of rabies vaccination, one can keep copies of hospital or doctor's prescriptions for rabies and complain to the police if needed.

8.6 Conclusion

As we saw in the surveys discussed in chapter 1, problems by kids and problems by the neighbor's pets were some of the major issues highlighted in the surveys. Addressing these issues with sensitivity, mutual understanding, and appropriate measures can help maintain harmony in the neighborhood. In the next chapter, we will discuss problems related to trees and plants.

Chapter 9: Problems Related with Trees and Plants

Disputes over trees and plants are common in residential areas. Overgrown branches, encroachments, or damage to property caused by vegetation can lead to conflicts between neighbors. This chapter explores these issues and provides practical steps to address them.

Figure: Damaging one's potted plants. Generated by OpenArt.ai

9.1 What to do if the neighbor damages or cuts off our tree(s) or potted plants without our permission

If a neighbor cuts down your trees or potted plants without permission, we can do the following:

1. Try to amicably resolve the issue with your neighbor. This is best to avoid costs. Have a direct meeting with the neighbor or with a mediator, explain your view of the

situation, also mention an estimate of the costs and damage they have caused. And get them to agree this will not happen again.

2. File a police complaint with any evidence if available (Such as CCTV, if a CCTV camera was installed in the garden)

3. Approach the tree officer: As per Indian law, nobody can cut trees (even their own trees, in fact) without the permission of the tree officer. Therefore, file a complaint with the tree officer in your area, which is typically connected to the District Magistrate (DM) or the SDM Office with details of the complaint. For example, in Delhi the tree department website is https://forest.delhi.gov.in/forest/contact-us and the phone number of the control room for the Delhi Forest Department is +911123378513.

4. Construct a Barrier: Install a high boundary wall or fence to prevent future encroachments.

5. If the police and/or SDM do not take adequate action, one can file a suit in the court asking for injunction to the neighbors from cutting or damaging any trees and if needed, asking for relief including damages.

6. If the neighbor makes any threats, try and record all such threats.

Note: all the above also hold if they damage the plants indirectly by cutting off the water supply.

In addition, potted plants and small plants in one's private garden are considered as property, and complaint can be lodged for damage of property before the civic court, before the police, before the magistrate, the SDM or forest officer. The exact person(s) to complaint to and the nature of the complaint can vary depending on the extent of the damages incurred.

Note: It is always better to collect proper evidence of the damage (such as photos, videos, CCTV evidence etc) before lodging any complaints.

9.2 What to do if a neighbor's overgrown trees are crossing over to the boundary of our property

If the overgrown trees or hedges cross over to our property, we can do the following:

1. If it's a minor growth, just trim the hedges
2. Try to resolve the issue amicably
3. File a lawsuit asking them to cease and desist their overgrown trees
4. File an application to the tree officer such as SDM complaining about the neighbor's trees
5. Install a boundary wall that is high enough

9.3 Obstruction of Sunlight or View

Sometimes, neighbors' trees or plants may block sunlight or scenic views from your property, which can be a source of contention.

Steps to Resolve:

Negotiate: Politely request the neighbor to trim their plants or trees to address the obstruction.

Seek Mediation: If direct communication fails, involve the housing society or RWA for mediation.

Legal Recourse: File a complaint with local authorities or approach the court if the issue significantly affects your quality of life.

9.4 Conclusion

Disputes involving trees and plants can often be resolved amicably through communication and mutual understanding. However, if the issue persists, legal remedies are available to protect your property rights.

Chapter 10: When Neighbors Make False, Unsubstantiated Allegations to Harass You

In a civilized society, disputes between neighbors should ideally be resolved through dialogue and mutual understanding. However, some individuals resort to making false and unsubstantiated allegations as a means of harassment. These allegations may be about noise disturbances, illegal activities, property violations, or other fabricated claims intended to cause distress.

False allegations can have serious consequences. They may lead to unnecessary police interventions, legal troubles, damage to one's reputation, and immense mental stress. In this chapter, we will explore why neighbors make false allegations, the impact of such claims, and the legal and practical steps you can take to protect yourself.

10.1 Understanding the Motives Behind False Allegations

When a neighbor makes false accusations, their actions are often driven by an ulterior motive. Some common reasons include:

- **Personal grudges** – Prior disputes over property, parking, or noise may lead a neighbor to fabricate complaints out of spite.

- **Attempt to intimidate** – Some neighbors use false allegations to create a hostile environment and pressure the other party into moving out or selling their property.

- **Land and property disputes** – Allegations may be part of a larger strategy to encroach on property, force a sale, or prevent rightful access.

- **Psychological or personal issues** – In some cases, neighbors who make false allegations may have personal insecurities, control issues, or a pattern of troublemaking.

Recognizing these motives early on can help in responding appropriately.

10.2 The Impact of False Allegations

Being falsely accused by a neighbor can result in several consequences, including:

- **Repeated police or municipal complaints** – The accused may face frequent visits by authorities investigating baseless complaints.

- **Damage to reputation** – If neighbors spread rumors or file public complaints, it can affect social relationships in the community.

- **Legal trouble and financial costs** – If false accusations lead to legal action, it may involve hiring a lawyer and spending time in court to clear one's name.

- **Emotional stress and mental health issues** – Ongoing harassment can cause anxiety, distress, and feelings of helplessness.

The key is to take early action before the situation escalates.

10.3 Steps to Take When Facing False Allegations

Step 1: Stay Calm and Avoid Direct Confrontation

When faced with a false allegation, it is natural to feel angry or frustrated. However, it is crucial to remain calm and not react aggressively. Any emotional outburst may be used against you by the accusing neighbor.

Step 2: Document Everything

Gathering evidence is critical in proving the falsehood of the claims. Keep records of:

- All written complaints or notices from authorities.

- CCTV footage if available, to disprove any allegations.
- Audio or video recordings of interactions, if legal in your jurisdiction.
- Witness statements from other neighbors who can testify in your favor.

Step 3: Respond in Writing to Any Official Complaints

If you receive a formal notice from the police, housing society, or municipal authorities regarding a complaint, respond in writing. Clearly state that the allegations are false and provide any evidence to refute the claims. Keep copies of all correspondence.

Step 4: File a Counter-Complaint for Harassment

Under Indian law, harassment through false allegations can be addressed by filing a counter-complaint.

- **Section 182 of the Indian Penal Code (IPC)** states that making false complaints to public servants is a punishable offense.
- **Section 499 & 500 of IPC** deals with defamation if the false allegations harm your reputation.
- **Section 503 of IPC** addresses criminal intimidation, in case threats are involved.

A written complaint can be filed with the local police or Resident Welfare Association (RWA).

Step 5: Seek Legal Recourse if Allegations Persist

If the false accusations continue, you may consider legal action:

- **Send a legal notice** to the neighbor demanding that they cease making false allegations.
- **File a civil defamation case** if the accusations have led to significant damage to your reputation.
- **Approach the courts for an injunction** to prevent further harassment.

10.4 Mediation as an Alternative Approach

If the issue is not severe but is causing distress, mediation can be a practical alternative.

- RWAs and housing societies often have grievance redressal mechanisms.
- A neutral mediator, such as a community leader or legal professional, can help in resolving disputes amicably.

This approach is particularly effective when both parties still have to live in close proximity.

10.5 Preventive Measures to Protect Yourself in the Future

To avoid being targeted by false allegations again, take proactive steps:

- **Install CCTV cameras** at entry points to have video evidence if needed.
- **Limit interactions with the problematic neighbor** to avoid unnecessary conflicts.
- **Build a good rapport with other neighbors** so they can vouch for your character if needed.
- **Document all interactions related to disputes** to establish a history of harassment.

10.6 Conclusion

False allegations by neighbors can be distressing, but a strategic approach—staying calm, gathering evidence, and knowing your legal rights—can help you tackle the situation effectively. While legal remedies exist, seeking a peaceful resolution through mediation or RWA intervention should always be considered first.

Living in harmony with neighbors is ideal, but when faced with baseless accusations, one must stand firm and take the necessary steps to protect their rights.

Chapter 11: Conclusion

In the previous chapters, we have explored various types of neighbor-related disputes, from noise disturbances and encroachments to issues with utilities, pets, and trees. We have also outlined strategies to address these problems, ranging from direct communication and mediation to legal remedies.

The Importance of Good Neighbor Relations

A harmonious relationship with neighbors can greatly enhance one's quality of life. Good neighbors contribute to a sense of community, mutual support, and security. However, conflicts with neighbors can lead to stress, reduce property value, and negatively impact mental and physical well-being.

Proactive Measures to Prevent Conflicts

While some neighbor disputes are unavoidable, taking the following proactive measures can help minimize conflicts:

- Open Communication: Build friendly relationships with neighbors and address minor issues early before they escalate.

- Community Engagement: Participate in or organize neighborhood events to foster a sense of unity and understanding.

- Clear Boundaries: Clearly demarcate property lines and responsibilities, especially in shared spaces.

- Document Incidents: Maintain records of problematic behavior or disputes for future reference, should escalation be required.

When to Seek Legal Remedies

Legal action should be considered as a last resort. It is often time-consuming, costly, and stressful. However, in cases of harassment, violence, or repeated offenses, seeking legal intervention becomes necessary to protect your rights.

As highlighted in Meik Wiking's The Little Book of Lykke, one of the keys to long-term happiness is having a supportive community where neighbors can rely on one another. Unfortunately, not everyone is fortunate to have cooperative neighbors. In such cases, understanding your rights and knowing how to address issues effectively can make a significant difference.

The hope is that this book serves as a practical guide for resolving neighbor-related disputes, improving the quality of life for individuals and communities alike.

About the authors

Siva Prasad Bose is a retired electrical engineer and writer of introductory guides on aspects of law in India. He is retired after many years of service in Uttar Pradesh Power Corporation Limited (UPPCL, formerly UPSEB). He received his engineering degree from Jadavpur University, Kolkata and has a law degree from Meerut University, Meerut and a BSc from MMH College Ghaziabad. His interests lie in the fields of family law, civil law, law of contracts, and areas of law related to power grid and other electricity related issues.

Joy Bose is a data scientist and writer. He has worked in the field of machine learning and artificial intelligence across multiple countries in Asia. He has co-authored this book with his father, Siva Prasad Bose, drawing on their shared experiences navigating neighbor disputes in India. His interest in practical writing extends to making legal and civic knowledge accessible to ordinary citizens.

Other books by Siva Prasad Bose

Introduction to Wills and Probate

Senior Citizens Abuse in India: And what to do about it

Introduction to Negotiable Instruments: As per Indian laws

Introduction to Marriage Laws in India

Managing Court Cases with Mental Strength

Self-Publish Books and E-Books in India

Delays in Court Cases in India

Introduction to Patents and Patent Law in India

Introduction to Property Law in India

Introduction to Tort Law in India

Appendix A: Glossary of Legal Terms

The following legal terms are referenced throughout this book. Understanding these terms can help you communicate more effectively with lawyers and authorities.

Adverse Possession: A legal doctrine under which a person who occupies another's land openly, continuously, and without the owner's permission for 12 years may acquire legal title to that land.

BNS (Bharatiya Nyaya Sanhita): The new criminal code enacted in 2023 that replaces the Indian Penal Code (IPC). Many IPC sections are retained in revised form under the BNS.

Civil Trespass: An unlawful entry onto or occupation of another's property without threats or violence. Remedied through civil courts and tort law.

Consumer Forum / Consumer Court: A quasi-judicial body set up under the Consumer Protection Act to resolve disputes involving consumers and service providers, including housing societies.

Criminal Trespass: Trespass involving intention to commit an offence, or to intimidate, insult or annoy the owner. Dealt with under IPC Section 441 / BNS.

DCP (Deputy Commissioner of Police): A senior police officer in charge of a district. Can be approached when local police are unresponsive.

Defamation (IPC 499-500 / BNS): Publishing or speaking false statements that damage the reputation of a person. Includes both libel (written) and slander (spoken).

FIR (First Information Report): The formal written document prepared by police when they receive information about a cognizable offence. Essential for initiating police action.

Injunction: A court order requiring a party to stop doing something (prohibitory injunction) or to take a specific action (mandatory injunction). Commonly used in property and nuisance disputes.

IPC (Indian Penal Code): The primary criminal code of India, now largely replaced by the Bharatiya Nyaya Sanhita (BNS) from 2024.

NC Complaint (Non-Cognizable Complaint): A complaint for offences where police cannot investigate without a magistrate's order. Used for minor disputes.

Public Nuisance (IPC 268 / BNS): An act or omission that causes harm, danger or annoyance to the public or to people in the vicinity.

RWA (Resident Welfare Association): A registered body representing the interests of residents of a housing colony, apartment complex or gated community.

SDM (Sub-Divisional Magistrate): A government official with quasi-judicial powers over a sub-division. Can handle complaints about encroachments, trees, and senior citizen protection matters.

Tort: A civil wrong that causes harm or loss to another person, giving rise to a claim for damages. Includes trespass, nuisance and negligence.

Appendix B: Quick Reference — Who to Contact for Common Problems

Use this guide as a first reference when faced with a neighbor problem. Always try peaceful negotiation first, then escalate as needed.

Excessive Noise (Late Night / Parties)

First: Speak to neighbor directly or via WhatsApp.

If no response: Complaint to RWA / housing society.

Escalate: Call police on 100 / 112.

Legal basis: IPC Section 268 & 290 / BNS; Noise Pollution Rules 2000.

Illegal Encroachment or Construction

First: Document with photos/CCTV; speak to neighbor.

Escalate: Complaint to municipal corporation (MCD, Nagar Nigam, etc.).

Legal: File complaint at police station; file civil or criminal suit.

Urgent: Apply to court for stay/injunction against further construction.

Electricity Theft or Tampering

Call your electricity provider (BESCOM, BSES, DISCOM etc.) to send a technician.

File complaint with electricity board online or in person.

Call police on 100/112 if supply is cut maliciously.

Legal basis: Section 135 of Electricity Act 2003.

Water Theft or Supply Disruption

File complaint with Jal Nigam / Jal Board in your city.

Call police if water is cut off maliciously.

Legal basis: NGT directions on potable water theft.

Threats or Violence

Call 100 / 112 immediately.

File FIR at local police station.

For senior citizens: Call 1090 / 1291 or senior citizens cell.

For women: Contact NCW; women's cell at local police station.

Legal basis: IPC / BNS Section 506 (Criminal Intimidation); Section 425 (Mischief).

Trespass on Property

Document with photos and witness statements.

File police complaint; file civil suit for possession.

Act within 12 years — do not delay or risk adverse possession.

Legal basis: IPC Section 441-447 / BNS.

False Allegations by Neighbors

Stay calm; document all evidence to disprove the claim.

Respond in writing to any official complaint or notice.

File counter-complaint if harassment continues.

Legal basis: IPC Section 182 (false complaint); 499-500 (defamation).

Kids and Pets

Speak to parents/owners first; be sensitive and calm.

Escalate to housing society / RWA if needed.

For pet bites: See a doctor; report to Animal Welfare Board if needed.

Legal basis: Prevention of Cruelty to Animals Act 1960 (for pet-related issues).

Trees and Plants

Negotiate first; trim branches that cross your boundary.

Complaint to tree officer (SDM Office / Forest Department) for unauthorized tree cutting.

Apply to court for injunction if needed.

Important Emergency Numbers

Police Emergency: 100 / 112

Women's Helpline: 1091

Senior Citizens Helpline: 1090 / 1291

Child Helpline: 1098

National Consumer Helpline: 1800-11-4000

www.ingramcontent.com/pod-product-compliance
Lightning Source LLC
Chambersburg PA
CBHW040517220526
45473CB00012B/2894